M000287928

LEARNING TO LOVE A WESTERN SKY

LEARNING TO *Love* *A* WESTERN SKY

AMELIA DÍAZ ETTINGER

Airlie Press
PORTLAND OREGON
2020

Airlie Press is supported by book sales and grants, by contributions to the press from its supporters, and by the work donated by all the poet-editors of the press.

P.O. Box 68441
Portland OR 97268
www.airliepress.org

email: editors@airliepress.org

Cover Art: August Macke

Cover and Book Design: Beth Ford, Glib Communications & Design

First Edition
ISBN: 978-1-950404-04-9
Library of Congress Control Number: 2019957029

Printed in the United States of America

To all my families and mountains.
All my loves from Cordillera Central to Mt. Emily.
And, of course, to my
steadfast love, my Chip.

Home is the sailor, home from sea,
And the hunter home from the hill.

—Robert Louis Stevenson

Contents

LEARNING TO *Love*

A WESTERN SKY

Patria

My dear beloved:

Describe
Patria
Homeland... too formal.
Country... no warmth.
But Patria is
family
food
colorful hands.
I shudder
naming your towns
Lares
Aibonito
Boquerón
y Caguas.
Sí, it is always Caguas.

I long to see your beaches
your red soil
feel your hot breath
against my shoulder
to smell pasteles wrapped in
green hope and
plantain leaves
to kiss my wise old man
and pet your boney dogs.

I long to feel the mildew of the Caribbean
filter the marrow
of cell
cement
and memory
to recall your loudspeakers
shouting
promise
and despair.

I long to feel that languid sun
extreme
suffocating
rapturous
transforming our men
arrogant and loud
with desires beyond
your narrow width
who dance and drink
love and think
with the intensity of your sky
that limits nothing
who wear guayaberas
and play dominos
and make love
with just a look.

Your mothers and girls
humble and strong
who run time
in heels and steel
making
and marking
keeping you afloat
in the perfume of rightfulness
in full lips that whisper
a future as uncertain as an eyelash
but make you believe
in god and children
and that there is no other
Earth.

Beloved Patria:

How is it to be you?
Especially now
when your children flee
when your soil is left behind
in empty lots
that hum
lost verses
of a mute song in a Caribbean
breeze.
This song of farewell.

Puerto Rican Diaspora

for those that fled or stayed
this became an endless tug-of-heart
where each accuses the other
for the desolation in the buildings once filled
with voices now boarded and hollowed
for dreams broken and sights discarded
and still we are all the same
we want bread sex and voice
along with the music we yearn
that reverberates in the bones of our ancestors
this Ocean makes us brother and sister no longer
we have become strangers
struggling to fit in oddly
if fitting at all
long lost verses seem to resurface
condemning blaming maybe redeeming
and yet the echo is heard in the look that says

"Traitor!"   "¡Traidor!"

no one wins in this diaspora of our souls
eyes gone blind still search and blame
for kitchen tongue and remembrances
metamorphosing
yielding
to a trembling that threatens
and exults more fragmentation
there are no absolutes except for the money
to fill our wants

the hemorrhage leads to less and less
but then
the streets are no longer paved in gold
no primary truths
but for our voices which vibrate identical
co-joined by indiscriminate birth to an island
now ripped separate by our human necessity
no redemption to be found in the exodus of despair
or holding the soil together with the faith of tree roots
maybe only in the rewriting of our new divided history

we take this to our own choice
if we stayed
if we left ...

San Juan's Night

On a different ocean
my children dance
hands enveloped in foam.
Their rhythm is a moonbeam
from youth.
My son with wonder yells,
Mom look!
In the black horizon we see
a night whale breaking surface
calmness among the carnival.

Silence at the Mozote

El Salvador, December 11, 1981

Maybe even the birds lifted in a vacuum
no rustle of leaves or feathers in the wind
when the women's skulls opened
like pomegranates under a tropical rain
of bullets.
Snakes and lizards scurried
over muffled bodies.
The last remaining
mother, whose pools of deep mahogany
never blinked or closed, stood
ankle deep in the blood river
while her breast dripped with untasted milk
when she entered those communal red waters.
In the other room, no sounds were heard
as heads of men fell side
by side from the toothless grin
of the machete. Quiet as a ripple
the muscles of fallen men vibrated
as evening entered through
the eyes of the house.
The callused feet of children
followed one another.
Never speaking
or touching, they huddled
as cold joined them to the others

while crickets sang.

Born of Ignorance

—or fear
a constant motion like waterboarding
laughter from a misspoken word ...
But words like evil water flow
over river rocks and open hearts
contours soften, sharpen, or disappear
eddies swirl on our surfaces
shaping character or dissolving essence.

These daily drips
sound innocent as rain,
but in time,
you taste
the iron in your blood
the salt of swallowed words.

The shape can become hard,
solid. Then the new self emerges,
but sometimes the edges sharpen
a serrated poison knife.
Then the heart wishes
it was the river rock.

Drowning in a Foreign Tongue

Do you know how it is to scream
against the scandal of ocean waves
tearing your lung—an invalid pen—
from the force of Anglican consonants
that weighs the tongue like foam
inarticulate,
that starves you to emaciation
suffocating noble feelings with
no voice, no resurrection
filling the space with
the grace of eloquence long lost?

Día de los Muertos

Dew covers this gray day,
light struggles to reach ground,
but cold has no trouble
filling space with living remains.

Cold whispers its name
at night in the coyote's call.
At dawn the bugling elk,
the slowing heartbeat of a dying friend.

Autumn of fog. The meadow
covered by a smoke screen of images
so real— father and child
in an eternal dance.

Their forlorn silence tastes
of mold, incense, and marigolds.
There are no altars this far north,
no carpets of yellow petals to lead the way.
Could they find their way?

Cold then becomes the friend,
a blue enduring hand
that sits and stills a shoulder.

Dew now descends. The maple, home, and fur
give rest.

Genocidal Stellar Dance

The scientist wrote:
"Locked in gravity
madly whirling
Neutron Stars inexorably
their partnership spiral
inwards
into a frenzied embrace
whose tempo quickens
tugging at each other
s t r e t c h i n g
their already amorphous shapes
touch, like Judas's
embrace and coalesce."

Unconsciously, he said "suicidal-stellar,"
unlike the tango's sultry dance
and yet reaching to be identical.

Genocide, whispered the tanguera,
her own tempo thickening, pulling
like gravity inexorably
a zarendeo spiraling inwards
she senses governmental documents
among coffee mugs and cigarette smoke
manly air thick, amorphous
s t r e t c h i n g
the frailty of it all
the last three minutes of her dance
a volcada with the power of annihilation
and she wonders if the astronomer
only sees a stellar dance.

Ode to Nicolás Guillén's Sensemayá

How would it be to hear the song that kills the snake?
Would it be the whistle of goat hoofs spinning on a dancer's neck?
The sounds of distant drums from your glorious pen?

Sensemayá!
Sensemayá!
Generations

follow your path. To the snakes.
Your rhythm forged in África.
Your yearning light that makes roots

bite the red soil.
And the grass to hide the snake.
The land, the music, the food of your forefathers,

balm of Cuba in every stanza!
Your words a gift to el Caribe negro,

now cast in mortar and steel.

Could this Caribbean see the snake's glass eyes?
Hear, Mayombe-bombe?
Sing your song to kill the snake?

Mayombe-bombe!
Mayombe-bombe!
Mayombe!

Last Night

Returning to youth
across dark fog
the distance is long
and the foot falters.

Open the iron gates
rusted by dreams,
a motherless girl playing alone.
Her hair luminous.

She has no eyes,
but shadows
for lashes
inert upon her cheeks.

Mouth red and round,
loose at its ends,
she cries.
At the bottom of the walk

there is a guava tree,
the girl sits in its lap sighing.
Her braids unmade
by a gentle breeze, she
stiffens her tender shoulders.

Thoughts hidden,
watching the fog lift
as the moment quavers,
she seeks solace
and climbs the fruiting tree.

Inside the Cradle

a motherless child lies
        clean hands
        combed hair
        no speech.
Under her eyelids that tremble
she forces a gate of light
into the night.
With her desire she beacons
        —a quiet face
        —a known smell
to bring a small smile
as her own soft arms
wrap around herself.
She can now exhale.

Youth in the Gym

A gray woman undressed,
her skirted bathing suit
a crumpled garden underfoot.
She reached for the towel and froze,
an Athenian statue of draped flesh
one un-manicured thick hand searching in circles
on her downcast-like-prayer breasts.
Her knowing fingers like hounds explored
Tierra incógnita of thin space and crumbled paper.
Finished, she sighed and grabbed a towel.

The young woman froze,
        —The old concern with health.
Her hands went to her breasts like magnets
confirming firmness and strength anchoring roundness
—not ready to let go.

Night Watch

No candlelight,
the air has no warmth
only the tick and tack
punctuates
the thoughts
of early night.
Outside the street seems calm
though there are some homes
alive in light.
This yearning lingers
for a time
where waiting in darkness
has no part.

Today

February 25, 1981

Oh, please don't let this moment go
our lips soft and wet
a fullness smooth as grapes.
Bathed in early sun,
your strands resemble gold
lost in my mane of brass.
My skin so tightly wrapped
around your young man shape.
Both wanting this time to hold
for we are afraid of growing old.

Today Talks Back

April 4, 2017

Ah,
the silliness of youth
to worry about rhyme in lips
and skin.
Today my graceless neck turns
to see the past
to find a void.
After all,
fear was not of age
or my brass turned to steel.
This lack of luster
in a kiss.
No.
The certainty is tomorrow
when there will be no touch.

Old Age

You become invisible.
A woman no longer desired.
But the body continues
the tendrils
the hypha
linger on a line
of sensuality
taking you underground
to the memories
of sexual abandon.
The maddening itch for touch,
incense,
and a cross to forgive you
tomorrow.
A night of surrender
without sorrow
that means nothing
except
to save you
from your own biology.

Phantasmagoria Allegro

She spends hours picking
lesions on her skin only she can see.
"See these bumps," she says again
and again, I smile. "No, I don't."
Silently we moisturize the crepe paper
of her hands. She has injured herself.

"Look out the window," I say, for a distraction.
"Those ropes," she points out, "Look!" she commands.
I look.
"Those boys, so industrious," she says with pride.
I puzzle at her ownership of a mirage.
"They spend hours on those ropes, walking on those trees."

The tree has branches as thin as herons' legs.
"Tell me about the boys," I say, exhaling.
"There are three of them, hair like dandelions, wild as feral cats.
They work hard all day, climbing, climbing. Enterprising!"
She smiles openly.

Three sons
all blond as dandelions.
Suddenly, I see.

Melancholia

It sits like a rock with ragged edges.
Another world,
heavy.
Stronger than gravity.
Where shoulders sink
until the spine crumbles.
Taking a breath,
a herculean effort,
as if air is acid swallowed by the
smallest of straws.
Iron eyelids shut any light.
Nothing penetrates this force
of broken glass thoughts
that make life a swirl of blood.
Tension flows to fingertips
that tremble against
currents that paralyze.
Impossible to rise.
An amorphous mass
wanting to levitate
but circles and repeats.

Dysphoria

Sadness grows
a veil made of spider silk.
Suffocating.
Enveloping eyes
without color,
sunlight trapped.
Insects on a web.
No violence here,
just the quiet of a crypt
dusty, discarded
decomposing
into ash so gray
it coats the throat with thirst
beyond water.

Carapace

As soon as he appears, chitin covers my soft cells
stiffens them with a suffocating grip.
Crackling with every step.
Within the sound of storms
torrents of water
cascading
as if Lyssa had the rains
of a hurricane
pushing, pulling, pulsating.

Inside, I am not an arthropod
shell disconnected, discordant
with this soft mass
of gray clouds.
Nephele tricked again
on frail flame
that wants flesh.
This he will never know—
escape.
This carapace-like shell
grips my face.
There is no current for the liquid me
as long as he is present.

In Methuselah

This dream of mine keeps rehearsing
uninvited and unwelcomed.
It comes smoothly in a breeze
or in the silk of innocence.
It rocks me in its arms
as a lover's trade.
It tightens its embrace
to suffocate.
So, I let my vision scan,
worried with perspiration
at the truth I might find in it.
That which I never care to see
yet it will come again
tonight, and tomorrow in the dark
and again, I will fall into it
and I won't resist its grasp.

The Loveliness of Death

Off the bridge
without a sound
waters close
and then return.

Back to the center
without temperature
or notion

no in or out
no breath.
Black of perfection

no colors
or memory
or guilt.

No noise
no words
the universe gone.

As it was before
we were.
Just wait,
and then return.

Mystical Woodpecker

My binoculars are covered in pollen
—so, it must be summer at last.
And here comes that woodpecker,
the mystical one,
the one I invented for times like these.

His feathers are made of steel.
His beak is neither gold nor hope.
Pure bone on flesh
brings a sort of peace
in heat, dust, and sorrow.

I saw him again today
when with trembling hands
I raised my ringing phone,
that hideous Talthybius.
I could not answer.

I no longer listen.
Let time rip my bones apart.
For now,
I'd rather watch my imaginary bird
through yellowed lenses.

Where Does Anger Go?

Does it crawl like a mongrel
to feed and fester under skin?

Does it keep company
quiet as hostage?

Does it seek refuge
under fingernails

to travel through capillaries and seep
over tissue as a contagion?

Wherever it goes,
it keeps waiting.

Half a Décima in Grand Ronde

I see winter sledding softly.
Mount Emily greets the green
valley, kissing the ground with frost
and I return to see your lips.

Clouds roll onto themselves
as they begin the descent on
the Grand Ronde Valley
under our mountain.
The sky won't be a cornflower.
Your arms around me never were.
The top of the mountain is gone
asleep under a gray blanket,
we once held above all others.
All three of us lay dormant in this silence.

Winter is under that white sky,
no leaves left to see.
Colors exchange for lack of warmth,
reds and orange turn to dark gray.
Those words we exchanged
keep sledding into us.
The sky no longer holds its
blue, and the frozen soil is hard
with promises no longer true.

Her Husband's Hands

For Tití Ligia who asked me for this poem

She tells me they were,

"thick, calloused, soft, and gentle
hands as big as hemlocks
ever-present for daily dangers.

His hands moved
over oak,
minds, or papyrus
rhythmical in conversation.

Hands that touched
the tendrils of my hair.
Multiplied from two to a million
in our bed, which defied perimeters."

She smiles at me,
embarrassed.

"Those hands carried home
a shell, like for a snail.
The water of our dreams
every day till the end."

Her right hand rolls
a golden ring
on her left.

"I feel them on my shoulder
when there is a quiet sunset
or when I catch a fish."

Apocryphal Postcard

The postman with a promise
of kisses in ink
delivered directly onto my palm.
Me, still at an age where I thought I mattered.

Excitement erupted into streams of giggles
muffled only by the possibility of her postcard
in my hand.

Shiny. Gaudy. Colors of a foreign city.
My nose detects no strangeness,
only stamps more colorful than ours.

To turn a postcard takes courage.
In it you might see truths and devotion,
the raw edges of a heart in words.

> So, I inhaled deeply with closed eyes.
> Steady...
> then turned.

The words lie, flat in black ink
whorls of thoughtless calligraphy
minutiae of a trip, a vista, a different existence.

She wrote no words for me
only a reminder, "say hi to her."

Betrayal in Hunting Season

There is a smell of apples in the air
and the Tamarack
[the one you planted]
has sprouted yellow.

Autumn is inside me
with colors going sepia.
Orange and rust stolen
by her kisses.
Did she taste of honey and berries?
Certainly not apricots; leave me those.

The smell of apples in the air
and your reflection on water.
A leaf floats where your heart should be,
bringing back your hand in mine,
walking over a leaf mosaic in our step.
Was her touch as soft as our step was then?

The smell of apples in the air
brought your breath at my nape, where the hairs
escaped my ponytail and you whispered, "You and me."

Autumn has returned,
promising snow
to erase the smell of apples.

I Gave You This, My Happiness

as a piece of rice paper
for safekeeping.
Light and unpretentious,
transparent for its honesty.

You put it in your pocket
for a quarter of a century
and then,
as if forgotten,
you charred the edges
and crumbled the center.

I held your own in my hand,
divided it as seeds,
planted them day by decade,
covered them with the soil
watered them with my lips.
I saw them grow.

So, I was unsubstantial,
you were strong, no matter,
in the end
I blew like the rice paper ash.

The Cambodian Manicurist

For a decade or so
she has bent her head
like Jesus
over women's feet
cutting nails and cuticles.
She lived for five years
in a refugee camp.
At eleven she walked
six miles for a cup of rice,
her brother lost
to the Khmer Rouge.
She escaped
hunger, rape, and hope.
A world lost to her
like the children
she did not care to have,
like the family she did.
Today she speaks
in quiet tones of English
she tries
to master
as she beautifies
our toes.

Mormon Angel

"The angel had on a loose robe of most exquisite whiteness"

She wants to be
a box of mirrors
    to trap the light inside,
        her aura dimmed—
        her need—
        to conceal—

she holds
back,
hand on heart.
        Such light! —

While she walks in circles
a dancer on a pin
        Maybe the angel—
who struggles but smiles
        who turns her
        a caged bird—
slightly out of sight,
a bad photograph.
Maybe she knows
        she blinds—
it still seeps from
her,
light under
a closed door.

I watch
impotent
wanting to be
blinded.

The Chemist Thinks of Her Love

as an ionic bond
but wonders who does the stealing.
Their polarization evident from the start,
different levels and all that,
but worse when the relentless water drips
on their metal roof
a titration of gray.
Time supplies each color
in silent sighs and vacant glances.
A kiss with the substance of an electron.
Staring at her skin, the chemist wishes
the blood underneath would rush,
creating a magnetic field.
Would that bind him stronger?
Passion is real.
Orbits of energy releasing heat—
no light, but sounds
like ancients forgotten,
like the ether that used to inhabit the cavity
of bone and skin and void.
Covalence might be in other homes,
other sentences.
Carbon to carbon was not their destiny.
She plays with a mote of dust
and wonders at matter as it rises.

White Fir

Cambium gone
from generations
making her center

home.

She stands alone
and surrounded

living

on the generosity
of neighbors.
These young trees—
less experienced
phloem and xylem
strong
still time to be hollowed—
feed her sap,

a communal photosynthesis.

This richness under her soil
extends for miles
intertwined
by the power of hypha

the alien

that holds
each root in prayer
that makes this forest
whole.

This old fir
she stands.

Lies

rain
from
your
lips
with
each
drop,
a practice puddle forms

clawing at clouds
only to find mud
no light brought forth
from our former selves.
To yours I add my own.

Now we drown.

Loving You as a Game of Sticks

"I love you as certain dark things are to be loved, in secret,
between the shadow and the soul." —Pablo Neruda

For those five hours, your heart on ice
my mind reached to hold a game of sticks

when we were strangers
the first time you said you loved me
and I saw your irises were honey.

sticks fell ...

For those five hours
an intruder held more than your heart in his hand.
I know it is not there where you kept me, but still ...

sticks roll ...

     Your heart on ice—
The yellow on top
when I said, "The rabbit died."
Incredulous you looked at my belly
as we walked in Duke's forest, intoxicated
with a future uncertain as a thought.

     Your heart on ice—

more sticks ...

My own heart pounding
but choked by a coldness
buried within.

The operating theater saw an aging man.
A damaged heart.
But you had been a boy
running amuck in the high desert.
Climbing Jefferson
racing your Jeep,
leaving tire tracks on ancient lava.
Just a dash outside the law
your freedom lost to duty.

arteries cut—

two dark sticks roll ...

Words from vodka, hurtful as tomorrow,
escaped like balloons
beyond reach, where would that take us?

more sticks ...

The clock on the wall a metronome of tension.

an orange stick rolls beyond reach ...

Your blood circulates in a metal box.
Has his hand faltered while I waited?
An empty mannequin.
An artificial life without your truth.
People in gurneys, white coats —
could they see in your capillaries, your heart on ice,
your steady hand on our son's shoulder,
your bull-headed determination
in this fog of randomness?

the blue stick rolls ...

Five hours of vigilance for a life
              the times we falter
              the sticks we pick
              the ones we leave behind.

Give Us Our Daily Ecstasy

For isn't he a dormant lover
aroused at the warmth
of water and honey?
Ebullient stimulation of growth—
a foam of exquisite aroma
should have lain on Venus' feet—
Botticelli's loss.
Then, inamorato hands surrender
inside its generous amorphous
self
wet with giving,
each breath a promise,
passionate abdication.
With each toss and turn
clouds of white like sheets,
a feeling of flesh delivered.

Rest and grow.

Will it be a Cezanne
or a quiet Vermeer?
Shape forced by lovers' hands.
Passion consumed in fire.
For fire is the other side of life.
Exhalations send another relinquishment:
'the little death.'

The Joy of Cooking

Where does it start?
At the farmer's dry hands to the soil,
or the tendrils of young green life that cling
to dirt, surfacing as conqueror
at market?
With tubers redolent of ancient civilizations
dancing with sweet fruit
at the slaughter house, or
at piglets' first frenzy feeding
turned later
to crimson rivers of iron and fear?

Maybe at the skillet?
Onions, celery, carrots
       soffritto
Onions, carrots, tomatoes
       sofrito
Olive oil hot as appetite
sizzling water to vapor
escapes to your receptors
salty, bitter, sour, umami.

Allium self defense
a lacrimation assault worthy of a warrior
surrenders an opaque orb to a translucent one
like a saint's robes.
Ceremony to fanfare mixing
red, green, and heaven
for eyes, nose, and pleasure.

Is it science, art, or slaughter?
It is magic that unfolds
from dirt and sun
to tickle the palate,
deliciousness,
fingers, forks, camaraderie
smiles and slaying.

Titration of Winter, or
The Rhythm of Summerville

dressed in her bridal gown
Mt. Emily sighs upon
the Valley a cold cadence that waits
      a light, a moving lane, or just the present

renewed by a man blowing on his hands
      —he forgot his gloves
the John Deere tractor removes snow
at a glacial pace under the grayish sun
one lone elk standing ground
its fur a canvas for the snow

a child's eyes peek from under a coat
eyelashes gleam with frost
a cup of tea steams on an empty table
an elderly woman taps a window
the junco's desperate flight
as a flicker mocks
the horse cast down with his heavy blanket

a titration so precise
can only describe
a town so grand
so small
so white

Eclipse in Eastern Oregon

August 21, 2017

Our primal selves can be lost to modernity,
but millions stop to watch her path in the sky.

To a small child,
so recently transplanted from Ethiopia,

the sky sits familiar even this far from the equator.
Among his new family he is a prince

and to comfort them he wears the funny glasses.
The moon has shed her dress of white.

She is black and wears a royal flaming crown.
"Zero-Moon," he exclaims.

He knows her name.

Vulgarization

The old cowgirl rides up her mountain
on two fat wheels and wonders,
what happened to men in fedoras?
They seemed to be gone after Vietnam.
Cultured men, gracious, solicitous
lathered in cologne, disappeared
with the black and white TV.
Hosts with ties striving for the special chosen word.
—Walter Cronkite, the most trusted man in America.

She takes a long breath and sits at a picnic table.
At 6,000 feet her chosen town below looks so small.
With a hand over the panorama she can erase
the colors of this town, the chimneys' smoke, the quiet streets.
If she cries right now, who would hand her a handkerchief?

Fedoras and handkerchiefs lost in one small generation.
Grand Ronde kitchens still cook a homemade meal,
a sweet inhalation for the cowgirl. She wants to stop the exodus
of gallant words, the man addressing a nation.
— "It is not what you can do ..."

Her chest feels laden with muck, just as her tires.
Mud has hardened on them, but at least it is Mt. Emily's mud,
she thinks as she mounts her Trek
and swiftly rides back down to the valley.

Fifties Kitsch From My Tío Paco

(The man who loved me most)

Your Knight of Columbus image
turned from sepia to virtual white
the day you brought home the DeVille
pink, red, and chrome,
blinding under the Caribbean sun,
a jewel like my Barbie's crown.
The entrance to our town—
the man who loved me most.

Your arrival at the Plaza, a legend.
Street urchins yelled and urged others to behold
fins that scratched the skies.
Neighbors leaned from balconies, fingers pointed, mouths agape.
Triumphant arrival to Benitez Street
—Hail to Cesar's Cadillac! —
Your legions shouted, but didn't touch the magic mirror,
the lacquered finish of your flamboyant car.

You honked the thin wheel; I saw your smile,
mirrored on a double grill
ivory over metal.
"Let's go for a ride."
A dashboard that could inspire The World of Tomorrow
"Designed after the P-38."
We could see all the adoring eyes of the town.

Yes!
Nested in the nacelle of a jet.
"Hydramatic, power steering, power brakes"
In those new words and that new language
I hear your voice; I see your face,
no longer dimmed
but young and caring—
the man who loved me most.

N.C. —Before You Disappeared—

On runs after school
under incandescent sun,
you, stained the Catholic white
of your uniform.
The neighborhood pharmacy, so close to home,
an oasis.
Its air-conditioned interior, a safe cave
        away from your stepfather's eyes.
Reading behind the shelves:
Wonder Woman—and, of course, Superman—
until caught.
Laughing with the abandon of a girl, just thirteen,
mouth full of stolen candy.
Who else knew?

Your name scratched from morning roll call,
but whispered in the halls as a snake crawl.
Girls huddling in tight groups,
Floating stories with the density of a stone.
Your cascabel voice silenced,
forced to be a sister to your child.

Who will play the guitar at the student show,
or fill the barrio with your laughter?

ACKNOWLEDGMENTS

I want to thank the editors and readers of the following journals where earlier versions of these poems originally appeared: *Willawaw Journal, Avocet: A Journal of Nature Poems, Windfall: A Journal of Poetry of Place,* and *Tierra Incognita Anthology* (Bob Hill Publishing).

Thanks also go to the Grand Ronde Writers and the Blue Mountain Writers for their insights and helpful suggestions for these poems and their encouraging friendships.

Thanks to my editor-friends at Airlie Press, whose dedication and thoroughness have been inestimable. And to Beth Ford for her amazing artistry.

ABOUT THE PUBLISHER

Airlie Press is run by writers. A nonprofit publishing collective, the press is dedicated to producing beautiful and compelling books of poetry. Its mission is to offer a shared-work publishing alternative for writers working in the Pacific Northwest. Airlie Press is supported by book sales, grants, and donations. All funds return to the press for the creation of new books of poetry.

COLOPHON

The poems are set in Cormorant, a contemporary serif typeface inspired by the Garamond heritage, hand-drawn and produced by Catharsis Fonts. The poem titles are set in Special Touch, a hand drawn font from BLKBK foundry in Winnipeg. The section art is adapted from the work of the expressionist painter August Macke. Printed in Portland, Oregon, USA.